How to be an Outst

CW00847917

"The talent of success is nothing more than doing ....

well."

– Henry W Longfellow

During years of hard work, I've been given different advice on how to become outstanding. Through following some of this advice, and adapting what I have learnt to suit my own style, I have achieved outstanding status and maintained it. The fact is, if your students respect you and always realise their full potential, you are an outstanding practitioner. The ways in which this is done vary depending upon personality and style and you should adapt what you read in this guide to you and your students. Outstanding teaching does not always look the same, but outstanding results do.

What is important, and increasingly difficult to maintain, is a work-life balance. This guide is succinct so that the time spent reading it is worthwhile, reflecting its key message: Make sure everything you do makes a significant difference to the learning because there is no time to waste in this profession. As teachers, we need to be selective. So much of what we do counts towards learning, but that doesn't always mean we should be doing it. It is important to recognise what *really* needs doing and to know how to do it effectively; this guide is intended to help you to do just that.

The focus is on:

Creating a Purposeful Learning Environment

Establishing Good Relationships

Establishing Routines

Independent Learning

Interdependent Learning

Engagement

Planning

Assessment

Marking

Observations

Behaviour Management

Reports

Work-Life Balance

Having a Bad Day

Intention

Creating a Purposeful Learning Environment

"Believe you can and you're half way there."
- Theodore Roosevelt

Creating a purposeful learning environment starts with your very first lesson and continues with each and every lesson after that.

Value Learning

Ensure your students value learning, understand its importance and completely acknowledge the direct correlation between effort and results. Quickly dispel any myths that certain students do well because they're 'bright.' Make sure they understand that doing well is a result of hard work and a lot of effort. Affirm this many times over the course of the year, stating at every turn the importance of effort when achieving success. Use appropriate people who the students know (either locally or globally) as examples so that they feel inspired by your words.

Value the Subject

From the beginning, ensure your students know the value your subject can bring into their lives. Have a quote that reflects this; display it where the students can't help but read it every time they walk into the room (www.brainyquote.com). Provide examples of how your subject can be used in the professional world or how the skills it generates are useful in everyday life. Give concrete examples; use real people. It could even be the starter task at the beginning of the lesson. The more personal a subject becomes, the better the results because when we feel an emotional attachment to something we are more likely to become involved. If students feel a subject is of benefit, and you make it accessible, they'll put in the effort because they understand what it has to offer them.

Consistent Use of Positive Language

Do not underestimate this. Get this right and your effectiveness in the classroom will soar. Praise should always be a main focus, even for mistakes. Regularly thank students for moving out of their comfort zone and attempting something new, even if they get it wrong. People aren't successful because they don't make mistakes; they're successful because they have learnt from the mistakes they have made. Ensure your students understand this and are not fearful. This is key to maximising success in your classroom. Praise those who attempt higher level responses (relative to their ability) the most and, if a mistake is made, show the whole class how they can learn from it by putting it right, using very positive language. Before long, most (if not all) students will attempt more complex responses because they see the value of the learning produced by doing so.

A 'Can-do' Attitude

Promoting a 'can do' attitude makes a notable difference to learning. Pass the ownership of learning from you to them. A lot of students work under the misconception that how well they do completely depends upon the teacher. Make sure you correct this crazy thinking! Teach them how to be good learners (more on this later on). Show them that doing well is not simply a result of the teaching, but also a result of taking ownership of their learning. Regularly reinforce that a 'can do' attitude, perseverance and hard work are what produce good or excellent progress. Tell anecdotes about students who have done just this or use yourself as an example, explaining that if you approach a lesson thinking, 'this is too hard for them; they are not very good readers,' you limit your expectations and therefore limit what they can achieve. It is important to have realistically ambitious expectations.

Displays

All of the walls in your room could contribute to the learning. Display descriptors so that the students are clear about how to make progress. Make them easy to access (not too wordy or full of complicated language) and easy to read (i.e. suitable font and size). Have a working wall, a place where some of the students' up to date work can be displayed, as well as the key points that lead to progress. Maybe have some questions so that the students think about their most recent learning every time they see them. They can display answers using post it notes or you can use it as part of a lesson to check understanding of new concepts.

However you use the walls, make sure that they are informative. Be sensible about it though. Apart from the working wall (which you can involve the students in to save yourself time), display information which will be useful for the most time possible. Get students or support staff involved in putting up the displays whenever you can. By your desk, have some wall space dedicated to you – somewhere you can put your timetable, planning and important reminders.

Table Plan

Set up the tables in a way that suits your teaching and is also instrumental to good learning - make sure you can walk around them and have easy access to each student. The maximum number of students, all wherever possible, should be able to see the board easily. Horseshoes are good (if you have room) as each student faces the front, can work with a partner and is less likely to be distracted. If you have any support staff, make sure they can access the pupils they are focusing on without having to disturb others.

Equipment

Be prepared. From the start, have all that you need for your lessons. You need to demonstrate to the students that your room offers all that is needed for great learning to take place. Keep it tidy and organised, demonstrating the importance of taking pride in anything to do with learning.

Supporting Each Other

Make sure the students understand the value of helping each other. This helps to create a positive and purposeful buzz in the room. Teaching others consolidates knowledge so encouraging students to help each other is a great way to cement learning. Not only that, it encourages understanding and respect.

If a student is finding something challenging, encourage them to look for a solution the following way: firstly by using their resources, secondly by asking their talk partner and thirdly (if they still haven't figured it out) by asking you. This encourages both independent learning and a supportive learning environment.

Remember:
Value Learning
Value the Subject
Consistent Use of Positive Language
A 'Can-do' Attitude
Displays
Table Plan
Equipment
Supporting Each Other

Once established, keeping a purposeful environment requires a consistent approach, one that demonstrates you completely buy into what you do and which ensures every lesson leads to progress. Your students need a purposeful learning environment in order to thrive. It starts on day one. Follow the points above to get this right and you'll have firm foundations to build the rest of your practice upon.

Establishing Good Relationships

"Try to be the rainbow in someone's cloud."
– Maya Angelou

Good relationships are essential, but, as we know, it's easier with some than others.

Suss out the 'Tricky Ones'

Work out what gets the trickier students on side very early on and then get them on side. Spend some time with them; get to know them. Ask them to do jobs for you, give them some responsibility, talk to them about life (or football) and eat lunch with them - anything that helps establish a good relationship conducive to a good learning attitude. Although this sounds a lot to begin with, it will help you hugely and save you a lot of time and effort in the long run. These students tend to carry a lot of influence and are important to win over from the start. Once you do, the right conditions for learning are established not just for them, but also for others in the class who'll no longer be distracted by, or pulled into, disruptive behaviour.

Ask Why

Quite often we forget to ask why someone isn't working or is being uncooperative. When we do, problems can be halved and misunderstandings can be avoided. It might not always be appropriate to talk during lesson time so make sure the student knows when he/she can talk to you. Knowing that you care can go a long way even if the student decides they don't want to share what is bothering them. After all, we are all on the same side. Remind students of this as it can be forgotten and, for some, not even realised in the first place.

Be Consistent

From the start, have very clear boundaries and high expectations. The students need to know what you will and won't accept and what the consequences are for anyone who refuses to act within that. Discuss why the boundaries are there (i.e. not because you enjoy dishing out consequences but because, in order for everybody to realise their learning potential, the conditions have to be right).

Make sure the students appreciate that the environment has to be conducive to good learning, one where everyone understands how it works and why it works that way (and that you are creating it for them). It is therefore in everybody's best interests to act within the boundaries. For example, it's important that all realise the importance of having respect for each other, not shouting out answers whenever they feel like it or interrupting the teaching and learning in any way. (That said, it is a good idea not to spend more than a few minutes laying out the criteria of good behaviour for learning because, if you spend too long explaining, it can start to feel like a declaration of war rather than high expectations.)

A 'No Hands Up' Policy

'No hands up' is good for nurturing a respectful environment (and keeps everybody on their toes). It takes a while to get used to, but gives everybody the opportunity to contribute as opposed to the few who constantly raise their hand and tend to always get picked. It gives everybody more of an even playing field. Give the students 'pair share' time (thirty seconds) to discuss an answer, but then keep complete power of choosing who answers by having no hands up. You'll find you can then hear from students you wouldn't usually hear from, improving the relationships and the learning.

Give a Little

One way to aid a good relationship with your classes is to offer some appropriate information about yourself from time to time. Just giving a little away can make you more approachable and, if they like you as well as respect you, it provides a fantastic environment to learn in. Just make sure it's still within the boundaries you've established, that *you* are still setting the tone, not the students.

A few years ago, I attended a course where a language teacher displayed a picture he always showed his students the first time he taught them. The room was silent as he explained that it had captured a very happy moment in his life. He was at his French pen-pal's wedding (they had written to each other since their school days some twenty years previous). He was laughing, a drink in one hand, an olive in the other and looked as though he was completely at home. It showed how his success at language learning had led him to the enjoyment of a life-long friendship and the opportunity to spend many happy occasions in another country, completely at ease with those around him, having the time of his life. The message was simple but very strong because he had personalised it. The personal touch makes a big impact on the students he teaches because they buy into the value of it, seeing how it has affected his life so positively. And they get to see him as not just their teacher, but also as a fellow human being.

Where is the Student Coming From?

It's important to consider students' experiences in their family and local community. I have worked in a variety of schools in affluent and poorer areas. Each required understanding as the students had different expectations, aspirations and experiences of consequences to actions. That's not to say my expectation of them was any different, absolutely not. But I had to adjust to their experience of the world just as much as they had to adjust to their experience with me. Otherwise, we would not have grown to understand each other (and I would not have been demonstrating that I was on their side). Students need to relate the learning occurring in school to their everyday lives as this serves as a powerful motivator to engage in their own learning.

Make the Extra-curricular Count

Extra-curricular activities (as long as they are not done begrudgingly) can make a big difference. If you're going to spend your precious time doing anything extra, it needs to be worthwhile and not just a box-ticking exercise. Choose wisely. Do something that either aids progress, enhances the kudos of your subject in some way, helps get the trickier students on side, addresses an area of weakness at your school or, if you're extremely clever, all of these things. Most importantly, pick something that interests *you*, it's more likely to be a success if this is the case.

Be Positive

Who wants to be with a teacher who constantly refers to the failings of the class? No-one. Positivity is crucial.

Make every student feel valued. Even when it is really difficult to find something positive to say, find it. When you have to speak to a student about non-effective behaviour for learning, always make sure you include a positive. For example, 'I know you're a mature person; I know you can make good decisions, so what's going on?' It takes out the battle that the student is expecting and reinforces that you have their best interests at heart. Now this may not work straight away. There are times when you know that a student is not in the best place to talk. Allow them some time to think and talk when it is better for them, again reinforcing the fact that you are there to help, not to punish. Avoiding the battles in the first place works better for everybody and, by building relationships in this way, the battles are less and less likely to occur.

Reports

Students read their reports and a lot of hard work can be undone if, after convincing them that you're on their side, you write nothing positive. Remember - your students are only young, learning a lot about life as well as education, and positivity goes a long way. It also makes you feel better. I'm not suggesting you lie, but always find a positive spin. For example, I had a student with many barriers to learning who needed a lot of support. When I sat down to write her report comment, I thought of everything positive that I could write and I used the word 'can.' I wrote that she '*can* be kind and thoughtful to her peers' and that she *'can* work well.' I pointed out an improvement in the way she responded to advice, stating that it was something she deserved praise for. This was not a lie. She was a student who found discipline of any kind challenging and had made progress with that, even though she was still not quite where the other students were. The positivity eventually came back to her behaviour in the classroom. She saw that I meant what I said, that I was in fact on her side.

The Word 'Yet'

Someone very wise advised me of the power of the word 'yet.' Whenever students talk about things they can't do, add the word 'yet'. I can't spell these words (yet!). I don't understand gradient of a line (yet!). 'Yet' changes everything.

Learn Names Quickly

Use names. Students want you to know who they are! Whichever student is last on the list when you try to write them out from memory is the one you could try to call home about, the one whose planner you could write a comment in and the one you could sit with in the dining room. Try to go out of your way to get to know the 'invisible' ones.

Always Greet the Students

As students enter the room, always greet them with positive body language using their names where possible; this sets a good tone for the lesson. If anyone looks out of sorts, discretely ask how they are. Find something positive to say to the tricky ones or quickly refer to something you know they are interested in (e.g. last night's football). If you've had a student behave outside of your expectations in the previous lesson, give a quick reminder (positively) about how they could maximise their learning potential. It's better to put in steps to stop the behaviour from happening in the first place rather than having to deal with the actual behaviour. Prevention is better than cure (as well as a lot easier).

Remember:
Suss out the 'Tricky Ones'
Ask Why
Be Consistent
Give a Little
Where is the Student Coming From?
Make the Extra-curricular Count
Be Positive
Reports
The Word 'Yet'
Learn Names Quickly
Always Greet the Students

Who was your best teacher? Not your favourite teacher, your best teacher? There may be a difference. Some of my favourite teachers were 'cool' or 'nice', but not necessarily the best teachers. Sometimes teachers make the mistake of viewing teaching as a bit of a popularity contest when actually, in order to create safe learning environments, you sometimes have to make unpopular decisions (rather like parenting). Reflect on your best teacher and use it to help you in your practice.

Take a breath before you react to any negativity. Whilst you take that breath, remind yourself that whatever it is isn't personal (even if it feels that way) and think about how you are going to react positively. It will make a difference.

Establishing Routines

"Success is the sum of small efforts, repeated day in and day out."
-Robert Collier

Be very clear from the start how you want things to work in your lessons.

Seating Plan

Have a seating plan and try to change it after every assessment to best fit the character dynamics and the progress. For example, it can be beneficial to sit someone doing well next to someone not doing so well so that skills can be shared. Some friends work well together, others don't. Figure this out early on and adapt accordingly. Always have your seating plan to hand because some students move themselves to see if they can get away with it. If the seating plans are pinned to a wall display board close to your desk (or in your planner if you don't have your own room), then this can easily be avoided. With primary classes, make sure that the students do not sit with the same people all day.

A Starter Task

Always have something ready for the students to do when they enter the room (preferably with an extension). It's important the students understand that this task will always push on their learning and that it's not just to keep them quiet when they come in. Link it to the previous lesson or the lesson they are about to have, depending on whatever serves the learning better. Vary the type of task so that it is engaging. Students should begin the task immediately because no learning time should be wasted.

Equipment

Be clear from the start what equipment you expect them to have and how it will affect their learning detrimentally if they don't have it. Decide on the consequences for not having equipment; tell the students what it will be, or decide it with them, and stick to it (although make sure they understand that the biggest consequence is, of course, less progress through lack of organisation). Have some equipment ready for repeat offenders to buy or borrow. You could ask the students for a small donation (five pence) to charity every time they rely on you for equipment.

Uniform

Make sure that students enter your room with their uniform worn correctly; high standards with this set the tone for what you are prepared to accept with everything else.

Remember:
Seating Plan
A Starter Task
Equipment
Uniform

When there is order, there is a sense of security and calm. Using the points above will help create the right circumstances for great learning. Be consistent with the students and, for the most part, they should be consistent with you.

Independent Learning

"A lot of people never use their initiative because no-one ever told them to."
- Banksy

Independent learning (also referred to as 'self-regulated learning') requires that students have a clear understanding of how to learn, that they are motivated to take responsibility for their attainment and that they work with teachers to structure their learning environment.

Teaching how to Learn

Teach the students how to learn. Introduce them to a range of techniques and explain why you are doing so. Encourage them to evaluate how effective each one is for them so that when it comes to them working without you, they know how to use the time most effectively to maximise learning. Promote the importance of active listening, applying previously learnt knowledge and using learning strategies taught in class. Do the same when it comes to revision techniques.

Memory

Students need to understand how to memorise information. This should be outlined. Dedicate some lessons to demonstrating different ways to improve memory - ways that are effective to store information not just in your subject, but in all of their subjects. The following link provides useful information regarding this:

http://www.rachelhawkes.com/Resources/Memory/Memory.php

Discuss the importance of sleep, exercise and diet on having a good memory. Some students do not realise that they are all connected.

Active Listening

Although students are in the room and sitting quietly, it does not always mean they are actually listening. If you see someone is thinking about their lunch or something other than what you are teaching, bring them back to the learning with 'are we all actively listening?' This should bring back focus and, if you use it regularly, your students will become better at staying focused on what you are saying. Alternatively, ask a question that the students have thirty seconds to answer on a whiteboard (make sure all students have the equipment necessary to use whiteboards at any point in the lesson).

Students must understand that it is not enough to just be in the room and sit quietly; they need to consistently process the words that are being said.

Problem Solving/Accepting a Challenge

It is too easy to switch off the moment something becomes challenging, to either expect someone else to figure it out, make an excuse or just not bother. This kind of defeatism needs to be addressed and combatted. Encourage students to see challenge as a way to discover new skills as opposed to a road to failure. Problem solving is an important aspect of independent learning as it encourages the student to really think and find solutions. Create these possibilities and praise the effort and persistence.

Praise

The kind of praise given is important. Always praise the effort, not just the result. For example, 'It is clear from this piece of work that you have tried really hard and you have clearly made progress as a result of this hard work.' If students know that their effort is recognised, they will be more inclined to put in the effort.

Self-evaluating

It is really beneficial to promote with the students the habit of reflecting on their effectiveness as a learner; encourage them to reflect upon their learning style and progress. Teach them to assess the quality of their work and how effectively they are using their time to learn. It's just as important for them to reflect on their performance as it is for you to reflect on yours.

Teacher/Student Partnership

Make sure the students understand that you provide the conditions for learning, but they have to do the rest. Progress is the result of effort.

Answering with a Question

Quite often, when a student asks a question, they know the answer but lack confidence in their judgement. In order to build confidence, answer their question with 'what do you think?' or 'you tell me' encouraging them to trust their own judgement and not worry about the risk of getting it wrong. They're usually able to give an answer and feel a sense of satisfaction when it's followed up with praise. Share really good questions with the rest of the class, praising whoever asked it and thanking them for helping everybody to learn.

Resources

Give your students a guide that includes the key aspects of their learning over the course of the academic year, with extra information for those that want to go further. This can be used in and out of lessons to enhance learning and accelerate progress. Create starter tasks that require the students to use it in a way that shows how valuable it can be (e.g. finding out certain information using the guide). There is evidence to suggest that students are more likely to remember new information if they've had to find it out for themselves. Tell the students this. Once the students realise what a difference it makes to their learning, they'll want to keep using it. This can also be used for homework tasks.

Purchase a good ICT resource that can also be used to promote independent learning. There are programmes which mark the work and keep track of how often the students are using it. For example: www.vocabexpress.com and www.mymaths.co.uk. Do some research and make a purchase. You won't regret it.

Interdependent Learning

Interdependent learning requires students to rely on each other to reach their objectives. When students support each other in their learning, great conditions for outstanding progress are created. Relying on each other for support and feeling satisfaction when others succeed is hugely valuable for both the students and for you.

Ways to Create Interdependence

Structuring tasks is a great way to create interdependence and there are many types of tasks that you could use to promote interdependent learning in your classroom. For example, assign different resources to different students so that they have to work together to meet the objective. Also, if the students work in groups, make sure each has a different role (without each role the group shouldn't be able to succeed). Furthermore, you could design tasks with cumulative contributions (for example, each teammate in turn adds a sentence to a team story). For more examples, visit www.kaganonline.com and look in the 'free article' section.

When evaluating a task in terms of interdependence, you should ask yourself: Is the contribution of one helpful to others? Is each contribution needed for the success of others? If the answer is yes on both counts, then the task creates interdependence.

Character Building

Supporting and learning from each other is not just important in terms of great progress, but is just as important when it comes to building good character. As teachers, we are relied upon for more than just our students' learning; we are also in a position to help mould their characters, encouraging and modelling good morals and values. Interdependent learning is not only effective for academic progress, but also for strengthening interpersonal skills, preparing students for the workplace where they will need to be able to work with others.

Remember:
Teaching how to Learn
Memory
Attention
Problem Solving/Accepting a Challenge
Praise
Self-evaluating
Teacher/Student Partnership
Answering with a Question
Resources
Interdependent Learning
Character Building

Were you an independent learner with the skills to work interdependently? Were you taught not just information, but also given the tools to expand upon it and effectively work with/support others? If you were, think about how this benefitted you. If you weren't, think about how this could have helped you! Either way, use the points above to make sure that your students know how to succeed not just in a subject, but in anything that they wish to pursue, using both academic and interpersonal skills. It is one of the greatest gifts you can give them.

Engagement

"I can't change the direction of the wind, but I can adjust my sails to always reach my destination."
– Timmy Dean

Have you ever been in a lesson where the students aren't buying into it? Was it clear why? Engagement is crucial and starts with how positive and enthusiastic the teaching is. You need to be convincing and for that to happen you must be engaged in the lesson yourself.

Planning

One of the keys to engagement is the planning. Plan lessons that excite you and that interest *you* as well as the students. Be creative. Don't be afraid to try something different. If it goes wrong, you know not to do it again. (After all, you are teaching the students this concept, right?) Don't always work from a textbook. Although it's easier, it can also be boring and put a ceiling on the learning. By all means, use a text book as a structure and dip into it from time to time, but plan tasks that use the independent learning resources. Use websites such as www.tes.co.uk or www.primaryresources.co.uk to help you find lessons and resources that have already been prepared.

Learning Styles

As much as possible, include different learning styles in your planning. When getting to know your class, figure out what works best with them. What do they best respond to? Ask them what works for them. Try to use sound and visuals as well as practical tasks.

Tasks

Always provide an extension. For mixed ability, provide differentiated tasks which the students can choose from. Allow those who believe they are capable of it to start with the extension, ensuring that you always have the next step ready in case they surprise you and finish with time to spare. In order to keep a good work-life balance, save everything you do clearly in labelled folders so that you can use it again. Once it's planned and resourced (as long as it worked well) use it the following year. Share ideas and resources with colleagues; it's always beneficial to discuss what others are doing. There's no point re-inventing the wheel, especially not with the time constraints in the teaching profession.

Use tasks that raise confidence; for example, those that (before tackled) are believed to be too difficult. Show, however, how it can be done. Attention will be paid because, along with everything else you have put in place (mainly the 'can do' attitude), your students will want to give it a go. Students will want to continue feeling successful in your lessons. For example, I've used foundation GCSE papers in year 8, making sure I give everything necessary for the students to be able to complete them as well as making it clear that it is most important to give it a go and learn from the experience. Once they accept this and try their best, they leave with a huge sense of satisfaction and a desire to do more of the same.

Stay up to Date

Keep up to date with new ideas and resources. Attend courses and read blogs/articles/reports that are relevant to you. Send links of useful tips to your colleagues. It'll help to raise standards and get you noticed for the right reasons. Some useful sites to look at are as follows: www.teachertoolkit.me (the five minute lesson plan that can be found here is a great resource), www.leadinglearner.me, www.thisismyclassroom.wordpress.com and www.createinnovateexplore.com.

Keep a record of the courses you go on, along with any notes taken so that you can provide them as evidence during your performance management review. (Tip: Start a performance management folder where you can save any evidence of performance development and save any positive emails you receive that celebrate achievement.)

What Interests the Students?

Try to be in tune with what interests the students and use this knowledge to enhance your teaching. For example, in some schools, ipads are used brilliantly to support learning and engage learners. If you have a sporty class, can you use sport in some way? Be creative wherever you can.

Teach to the More Able

One technique I highly recommend is teaching to the more able. It raises standards. No-one can just sit back due to the high level of progress it creates. Students engage because they know they are making progress and want to continue doing so. Not only that, they can't afford to miss anything because (if they do) they start to fall behind; they realise that each moment of the lesson counts. This is very powerful. However, be careful not to lose the lower ability; differentiate tasks accordingly so that they can access the learning. Have less challenging tasks ready and use any support in the room to cater for different abilities. The support does not always need to be with the less able; it can be directed towards the more able so that you can support those with particular needs. Do whatever works best for your students.

Value the Learning

As mentioned before, make sure the students understand the value of what they're learning. For example, I find in key stage three, the students do not always realise that everything they are doing is already important for GCSE. Make the link wherever you can, for example, display a GCSE question on the topic you are studying. Make the learning relevant to their exams and, wherever you can, to the world they are living in.

Adapt to the Class

If you sense the students are not buying into what you are doing, no matter how enthusiastic and well planned you are, then don't be afraid to ask why. Talk to them and, where you can, adjust. Nothing is set in stone, even if it is on a plan. As long as the objectives are being met, changes are fine. On one occasion, I had a less able set arrive and I'd planned for them to do an assessment. However, the learning support assistant informed me that they were not in the most focused frame of mind due to assessments earlier in the day. It was clear I had to change what I'd planned; so I did. I had a lesson prepared that I'd taught to a different class. I used that instead and did the assessment the following day. I told the class that I'd changed the lesson, reinforcing that we were indeed on the same side. They were grateful and did well in the subsequent lesson when they were much better placed to do the assessment.

Remember:
Planning
Learning Styles
Tasks
Stay up to Date
What Interests the Students?
Teach to the More Able
Value the Learning
Adapt to the Class

What was the most interesting lesson you ever had? Why? Tune into this. Speak to the students and tune into them. An engaged class is a pleasure to teach and an engaged teacher is a blessing.

Assessment

"It had long since come to my attention that people of accomplishment rarely sat back and let things happen to them. They went out and happened to things."
– Leonardo Da Vinci

Assessment is essential to get right, both in terms of pitching and frequency as well as recording and monitoring.

Frequency

This tends to be out of your control and fits in with the school policy. Always be very focused on the learning that needs to happen in order to succeed in the assessments and be aware of how much time you have to achieve it. Cut out the unnecessary and stay focused, ensuring the students know when and how they are going to be tested on the learning they are accruing. This supports the engagement and encourages independent learning because they know what to do in order to succeed.

Recording

Have you ever had the experience of a student being asked about their attainment and targets and they can't respond? One way to avoid this happening is to use a 'progress log.' Start a book which documents all of their assessments, progress and targets. On the front page put a sheet where they can mark the results of all their assessments and write their targets. On the inside front cover, put a progress ladder that the students can highlight and date regularly with their learning. Make sure the students know where it is so that they can always check their progress (go through it with them after every assessment) and, also, so that they can show it to anyone who asks about their progress. The evidence is always there and you have up-to-date data (as well as evidence of all previous attainment) on every student you teach. These can be passed to subsequent teachers and can be kept within departments. All of your data will be stored electronically on a school system, but it is very beneficial for the students to have a detailed record of their progress (and it does not take too much time to do). In order to maintain a work-life balance, students can stick in their assessments, update their progress ladders and write in their targets. You just need to mark the assessment and give it a grade, which you would do anyway. A sticker on the front of their class work book with the target level written on it is also a good idea.

Monitoring

Analyse the data from your classes and act upon it. Re-jig your seating plans. Place those doing well next to those who could do with a positive role model (making sure it doesn't have the opposite effect of hampering the progress of the student doing well, of course). If needed, organise some support sessions. To save time, consolidate the learning of the more successful students by using them to do the supporting. I have run lunchtime workshops in this way which have been really successful. I have been there, but able to get on whilst the learning is happening in the room. It is a delight to see happen. If you do this, note how it has affected progress and get some feedback from the students about its effectiveness. It's great evidence for your performance management review.

Peer/Self-assessment

This is an important aspect of assessment and could be in a number of sections in this guide. It serves as a time-management strategy and improves the quality of marking too. Allow students to assess their own work as well as that of their peers. It involves students more in the learning process and therefore promotes progress. Furthermore, it serves as a bit of a break for you. Be very clear about how they should assess; this may take a little training in the first instance. Bring attention to the marking in their books - the fact that all comments are constructive.

Remember:
Frequency
Recording
Monitoring
Peer/Self-assessment

Assessment is only effective if purposeful learning has taken place beforehand and if action is taken afterwards. Students should feel it's a worthwhile experience in order to see the value of preparing themselves well for it and feel secure in their learning.

Homework

"Don't mistake activity with achievement."
– John Wooden

Homework can cause a headache. First you have to figure out the task, prepare it, collect it in (chasing up those who have not completed it) and then mark it before the process starts all over again. In order to be effective and maintain a work-life balance, homework needs to be cleverly thought out.

Worthwhile Tasks

If it isn't pushing on the learning, there's no point setting it. The practice has to be purposeful. For example, you could set homework which puts the students in a better position for the next lesson: learning vocabulary, learning key facts, doing some background research (all of this becomes easier when they have the guide mentioned earlier as you don't even need to prepare any resources). Involve the students in the decision as to what they should do. Ask what they feel would be of benefit. If they have helped to make the decision, they are more likely to put the effort into doing it and doing it well. This accelerates progress in the lesson.

Minimal Marking Tasks

As well as the types of tasks mentioned above, set research tasks that the students can then share with each other and peer assess. Whatever you set, make sure that it's worth doing and won't take you hours to collect in and mark. For example, ask the students to respond to any comments you have written in their books. It should be understood that the biggest consequence of not doing the homework is a negative impact on progress. Make it clear that the students are doing it for themselves, not for you.

At a younger age (primary) or less able stage there is almost no evidence to suggest that homework increases progress. In fact, evidence suggests that students at this level do not learn by doing homework. It is much more important to keep them communicating with their parents about what they are doing and keep up the fun and enjoyment.

Record the Homework

Be organised with this. Both you and the students should have it clearly written down somewhere, preferably in planners. Also, many schools now have online VLE based systems, which are helpful as parents can see it. For the students, write a brief summary of the task, how much time it should take and the date it needs to be in. To begin with, check it is written in the planner before they leave the room. Avoid setting it to be completed the next day; you'll end up with a lot of complaints and reasons why it can't be done!

Remember:
Worthwhile Tasks
Minimal Marking Tasks

Record the Homework

Homework should be accessible, student led, easy to mark or require no marking at all. Make it work for you as well as for the students.

Marking

"No matter how good you get you can always get better, and that's the exciting part."
- Tiger Woods

Good marking makes a positive difference to progress and is important to get right for this purpose.

Regularity

Try to have a marking timetable. This way, you are less likely to end up with a pile of books that take you hours to mark because there is so much to be checked. However, if this does happen, be sensible. There's no point writing comments if the students have already moved on. Only write something if it adds to the learning otherwise just give it a tick to show that you have seen it (there should be at least a tick on every page). It's important that work is checked at a point where the marking can make a difference.

Keep the Books Open

When you take the books in, it sometimes helps to keep them open on the right page as it saves time looking for the work.

Comments

Effective marking is regular and shows progress from one piece of work to the next. Every comment needs to be worthwhile as time is too precious to do anything that doesn't significantly count towards progress. At the end of the piece of work, you could use 'WWW' (what went well) and 'EBI' (even better if). Write both and follow each with a short sentence. Alternatively, you could write 'T' in the margin and write a target or 'Try this' with a suggestion following it. There are many ways to give feedback. Be aware of your school's marking policy and then adapt it as necessary so that it works for you and your students. You could ask the students to look at their work and write their own target, involving them in the evaluation of their work. It is important that they are always aware of the next step and therefore know how to make progress. (Useful marking stamps can be found at www.schoolstickers.com.)

Student Responses

Ask the students to respond clearly to your comments in a certain colour (e.g. red). Give them time to respond, possibly set this as a homework task or the starter activity. Each time you mark, give their responses a quick tick to show that you have seen them or correct them as necessary. This kind of marking counts; it aids learning and ensures students take pride in the work in their books. Make sure all students understand that their books are a record of their progress and a reflection of the pride they take in their learning.

Highlighting

Use highlighters to save you time. For example, highlight spelling errors in pink and grammar mistakes in yellow. Explain to the students how to react to this highlighting. For example, if there is pink, write out the spelling correctly three times. If there is yellow, write out the whole sentence correctly (in red pen, of course). This cuts down on what you need to write.

Verbal Feedback

If you speak to a student during a lesson, make sure that you write 'VF' in the margin and circle it. Ask the student to write a comment about how it has helped (in red, of course).

Colour

Always mark in the same colour (e.g. green) and when hover supporting during a lesson, have a green pen with you as you walk round.

Limit the Work in the Books

In order to spend time effectively, only put work in the students' books where marking is essential to push on the learning. If what they are doing doesn't need to be evidenced for this purpose, use whiteboards or the back of their books.

Remember:
Regularity
Keep the Books Open
Student Responses
Comments
Highlighting
Verbal Feedback
Limit the Work in the Books

Establish a system that the students understand and stick to it, making sure that what is written in the books (by both you and the students) makes a significant difference.

Observations

" You must expect great things of yourself before you can do them."
— Michael Jordan

Observations offer the opportunity to show off your everyday practice. If you do what has been outlined in the previous sections, then it is something to feel very positive about.

Outstanding Over Time

Observations should be a reflection of your usual classroom practice, not merely a show for the observer. For your colleagues to be aware of your daily practice, try and adopt an open door policy. This can be intimidating at first, but it really helps to build confidence and allows others to see the work that happens in your classroom. If you only stick to three observations per year, how can a full picture of your day-to-day practice be constructed?

In order to receive the 'outstanding' grade, you have to show great results, marking that shows progress, well established routines, good relationships with students as well as top notch teaching. The teaching can be shown on the day, but the rest is evidenced over time. Believe me, if you have an obvious 'can do' culture in your classroom that is reinforced with positive language consistently linked to the learning (and you're teaching to the more able), your observer is going to leave feeling impressed.

Planning

It's essential not to overthink it. Planning should be clear and concise.

It should at least include:

Where the lesson fits into the scheme (e.g. previous learning and where the unit is heading)

Clear and concise differentiated objectives, graded where possible, that the students can understand

Differentiation (with names where necessary) and where any support is directed to (provide support staff with the plan before the lesson)

Modelling of the task (how much will depend on previous learning)

Literacy/Numeracy/ ICT

Assessment for learning – make it clear how you will assess the learning at various stages of the lesson, especially the end

An effective plenary that demonstrates progress

Homework

Make sure each stage of the lesson accelerates learning; always refer back to the objectives. The assessment for learning needs to be very clear so that you know that all are accessing and, if they aren't, you can address it. Two good strategies to check understanding are the thumbs up, sideways, downwards approach or mini whiteboards, allowing you to quickly judge where *all* of the students are at and what your next move should be.

Coming off Plan

Never be afraid to come off plan. If, for whatever reason, (for example, maybe in your willingness to impress, you've pitched too highly) the lesson needs to take a different turn, even if there is someone observing you, change it. The most important thing is the learning and if that's not happening, do something about it. Think on your feet and go with the flow of the lesson. For example, you may need to go over a crucial component of the learning more than you've planned to as the students aren't grasping it as quickly as you thought they would. Don't carry on regardless; do quick mini-whiteboard activities to make sure they are secure with the learning before you move on (this may only need five minutes). Good pace does not mean being fast, it means spending the required amount of time needed on each part of the lesson (not too much, not too little). This will then lead to and show progress, which is what it's all about.

You should know your students well and have a good idea of what works with them. If they are not behaving as they usually do, challenge them in a positive way. For example, 'Now, the learning in here over the last... has been excellent, what is going on today? How can we improve this to show what good learners we usually are?' This needn't take long; it's better spending two minutes getting the behaviour for learning right rather than an hour with it wrong.

Pitching the Lesson

It is essential to get this right and the success balances on doing what you usually do. If it's too easy or too hard, the students will switch off. Don't suddenly go for something completely different that throws the students off-guard. Follow on from previous learning at the high rate of progress already established, using effective strategies you've already embedded (see previous sections). Listen to your inner voice. If it's telling you there's something not right with the pitch of your lesson, there's going to be a problem with it. Change it so that you feel completely comfortable.

Engagement

You know your students and how they respond to certain tasks. Pick something they love to do. Choose a lesson that is particularly good at showing progress – one that uses/demonstrates previous skills and knowledge which are then added to significantly in the lesson.

All classes are different and can respond differently to the same task; make sure what you do is likely to be successful with the class you're teaching. It's not a good idea to pick a lesson that is more of a consolidation of skills, unless of course the learning is so good that it clearly demonstrates outstanding progress over time.

Make Sure the Students Work Harder Than You

One of the most common criticisms of a lesson is that it is too teacher led, although it is now recognised that this is not always a bad thing as, after all, the teacher is the expert in the classroom. That said, the students should be working harder than you and have plenty of opportunity to build upon or apply their learning. Never forget that it's all about the students. Try not to fear letting them get on independently. This is why the routines, the relationships, the recognition of the importance of your subject and the understanding of how to be good learners are so important. If these values are in place, the students are less likely to be off task.

Peripheral vision is essential. Always be aware of what is happening in the room, even when you are focusing on one student. Then, you can quickly put right anything that isn't working.

Look at your plan. Will the students be learning for the most time possible, either individually, in pairs or as a group? Limit your words to what is necessary for meeting the objectives and cut out the rest. When modelling a task, be succinct and check understanding before the task is started.

Differentiation

Clearly mark on your plan how you're supporting the most and the least able. For example, although the pitch of my lessons is to the more able, I have to be sensible about this. In two of my classes, I have fluent speakers. It would be ridiculous to pitch the lesson to their standard so I need to mark on my plan what they are doing. Some of the less able find the pitch a little high, so I also need to mark on my plan how I'm supporting them (e.g. sitting next to a more able student, hover-support, an easier task etc...). Provide support staff with a plan to ensure they know exactly where to be and what to do.

Visualisation

Try to visualise the observation going well. The positive energy generated from this will make it more likely! Don't overthink it; act as you usually do – on autopilot and trusting your instincts. When you start to question your decisions and over-think what you are doing, you will not be at your best. Don't be nervous, be yourself.

Feedback

Feedback should be given within twenty four hours. There's absolutely no point in having an observation without the feedback. None whatsoever. After all, how can you work on areas for development if you don't know what they are? You also need to be aware of your strengths. During the feedback, let it be known how the last observation affected your teaching – what do you now do differently as a result? How have you improved? Use the feedback from each observation to further your professional development. Evidence this for your performance management. Even with an outstanding lesson, there will be something to work on (save the written feedback for your performance management review).

Tell the Students

Let the students know that there will be a visitor in the lesson. Tell them that the observer is there to observe the learning and not to watch the teacher. Encourage them to show off what great learners they are, demonstrating the skills that they have learnt, taking risks and sharing knowledge.

Be an Observer

As often as you can, take the time to observe your colleagues. (Obviously, check with them first.) Pick out colleagues that are strong in areas you need to improve upon and watch them with that area as a focus. Make notes of what they do and apply it to your practice. Keep the dates and notes and use them as evidence in performance management meetings. If your school is open to it, have a walk round where you get to see lots of different teachers in action for short periods of time. You will then have the opportunity to see how your students behave in different lessons and you can pick up some good ideas.

Remember:
Outstanding Over Time
Planning
Coming off Plan
Pitching the Lesson
Engagement

Make Sure the Students Work Harder Than You

Differentiation

Visualisation

Feedback

Tell the Students

Be an Observer

As always, respond to the students and keep an eager eye on how they are responding to you. Stick to the objective, express it clearly at the beginning of the lesson, come back to it at the end and assess the learning that has happened in between. The rate of learning will depend not just on that one lesson, but on all that you have put in place beforehand.

Every lesson counts because it is, quite simply, all about the students. The best classroom is one where everybody is working together (like a coming together of great minds) to reach a definite aim. That's not to say that everyone works as a group on a task, but that they work together to provide a great learning culture. The attitude cultivated in their learning environment will be evident in every single lesson and come across in every observation. It is important to get this right from the start.

Try to acknowledge the benefit of an observation, seeing the experience as an opportunity to display your strengths and gratefully receive tips for further development. Believing this will help you to act as you normally do, rather than breaking into a hot sweat and over-thinking the lesson. Simply be yourself.

Behaviour Management

"Sometimes they're just not ready to receive your greatness, but that doesn't mean you should stop being great."

\- Anon

You can have the best teaching skills in the world, but if you do not have good behaviour management, your results will always be mediocre. Behaviour management is much easier when you have established good relationships; this, along with consistency, is essential.

Use Your Voice Wisely

Your voice is one of the most powerful tools when it comes to behaviour management. Use it wisely. Shouting doesn't work long-term, not really short-term either. Your tone always needs to communicate that you are in control, that you mean what you say. Sometimes, deliberately speak quietly and calmly; the students immediately engage as what you're saying seems very important, creating calm in the room.

When reminding students to work quietly, also remind them of the need for a good learning environment so that they can realise their potential – always bring it back to the learning. If someone calls out and interrupts you, pause for a moment. Continue once they've stopped. This works as long as it is done with confidence and is consistent. Vary your tone and volume to suit the behaviour in the room and always sound in control.

Don't Take Anything Personally

It is difficult sometimes to not take negative behaviour, such as defiance, to heart. It is too easy to think that it is our fault, that we should have done something differently. Well, sometimes this may be true, but let's not forget that this is no excuse for rudeness. If a student is behaving negatively, there is usually a reason that goes deeper than the teaching in your classroom. Do not take it personally.

Teaching is a profession that requires a lot of energy so channeling it positively is essential. Taking negative behaviour personally is not conducive to this. By all means reflect on the situation, but make sure you come out of it with a positive solution (reminding the student you are on their side/offering to help with whatever is bothering them/finding time to talk to them about life/asking why they are behaving in this way/talking to colleagues etc...)

Speak to your colleagues and find out whether a difficult student is displaying the same behaviour elsewhere. However, be careful not to enter into too much 'group venting' (where it is a case of just complaining), but seek solutions. Beware of the very unhelpful, 'Oh, he's never a problem for me,' type of response. Find out who has good strategies to deal with the issue and learn from them. Ask to observe them to see what they do.

There will always be students who are not in a place, for whatever reason (and there is always a reason, quite often nothing whatsoever to do with you), to accept any help you try to give and who are not ready to change negative behaviour for learning. In these instances display patience, don't give up, never take it personally and make sure you know who it is you need to refer your concerns to so that the student receives the help he/she needs.

Look for the Good

Always look for the good and focus on that rather than the not-so-good. For example, instead of 'Johnny, open your book and start working now,' try, 'well done George. That's a really great start and will help you make good progress.' The class will respond to the positivity.

One to One

If a student is being particularly awkward, always try to speak to him/her without the rest of the class as an audience. Some students love attention, good or bad, so make sure you only give it for the good.

The Look

Perfect 'the look,' one which is recognised as 'you need to listen' without the need for any words.

Use 'Thank You' Rather Than 'Please'

For example, 'underline the date. Thank you.' This conveys the message that you're expecting it to be done and, as they've already been thanked for it, they feel obliged to do it.

Give Time

If the previous strategies aren't working and someone is behaving in a challenging way, be clear about what you want them to do and give them time to take up the instruction. Walk away at this point, but make sure you give them a time limit (e.g. two minutes) and return at the end of that time to make sure the instruction has been followed. Once you've issued the time limit, the student should be aware of the consequence of not doing as you've asked.

Be positive wherever possible. If a student does not do as they have been asked, issue the consequence quietly and calmly. Shortly after the lesson, ensure you have time to discuss the behaviour in order to minimise the chances of it happening again.

Call upon Colleagues

Never be afraid to ask for help. There will be times when, through no fault of your own, a student is simply not in the right frame of mind to learn. If this is displayed through disruptive behaviour and, despite all of your best efforts, the learning of the rest of the class is being slowed down, call upon a colleague. It could be another member of your department/year group who simply allows the disruptive student to work in their classroom or, if more serious, a member of the senior leadership team. Either way, it is sometimes required and should not be seen as weakness on your part. Do not take it personally and always try to find out the reason(s) for the behaviour.

Involve the Students

When deciding on what is and isn't conducive to good learning, involve the students. Ask them what the consequences of negative behaviour for learning should be and ask/remind what the consequences of good behaviour for learning are (realising potential).

Parents

Involving parents is essential. Whether good or bad, it is beneficial to call parents and keep them informed of their child's attitude to learning and consequent progress. Again, be careful with your words; be as positive as you can. Make sure the student appreciates that you are making the call because you care about their progress and want them to do their best, not because you want to make life difficult for them.

Dress Smartly

Although what you are wearing shouldn't make a difference, it does. If you want to be taken seriously, make sure your clothes give the right message.

Lead by Example

Actions speak louder than words. For example, you can't expect the students to take pride in their appearance if you don't or the students to be prepared for lessons if you're not. They will take more notice of what you do than what you say.

Mean What You Say

If you say that there will be certain consequences to certain behaviours, make sure you see them through when the need arises. Students will lose respect if, due to a lack of consistency, they don't believe what you say.

Fairness

Always try to be fair. There are times when consequences may need adapting because of special circumstances. If this is the case, without going into detail, make sure that the students are aware that you have been fair and responded to the needs of the situation because you are always on their side. The students need to have trust in your judgements which is built over time by your actions and your words.

Remember:
Use Your Voice Wisely
Don't Take Anything Personally
Look for the Good
One to One
The Look
Use 'Thank You' Rather Than 'Please' ✓
Give Time
Call upon Colleagues
Involve the Students
Parents
Dress Smartly
Lead by Example
Mean What You Say
Fairness

Who did you respect at school? Why? Look at your colleagues - who do the students behave well for? Observe them and figure out what it is that they do. Use the strategies listed in this section, as well as any you pick up along the way, but stay true to your own style. Believe in yourself; show no doubt that what you expect to happen will happen. Young people will pick up on the slightest element of doubt within a heartbeat. Secure their belief in you with a secure belief in yourself.

Work-Life Balance

" The price of anything is the amount of life you exchange for it."
-Henry David Thoreau

Always consider whether the next task on the never ending 'to do' list actually counts for anything – will it make a significant difference to the teaching and learning? If it doesn't, cross it off the list.

Prioritise

Always try to do the things that others are waiting for first, preferably as soon as you get them so that you don't forget.

Never have more than five things on your 'to do' list for one day. This way, you have to prioritise; you have no choice. Also, you won't feel completely demoralised when you've not managed to mark one hundred books, plan for the next week, write reports, prepare resources or eat lunch. Instead, you can feel positive about the things you have managed to do.

Sometimes, we need to remind ourselves that there are only so many hours in the day and that the world isn't going to stop spinning because we haven't written next step comments in the workbooks for a week. The busiest times can be overwhelming. At these times, take a deep breath and a step back. Are the most important things done? Are the students still learning? If the answers to these questions are yes then the most important aspects of the job are right and you can take comfort from that.

Plan Accordingly

When you're incredibly busy, plan some lessons which require less of you but where the students are still learning. For example, use a good ICT resource to set tasks which push on learning as well as give you some breathing space. It's even better if no marking by you is involved. Now this can't happen too often but, every now and again, it's a beneficial way of dealing with the ever-increasing demands of the teaching profession. It's beneficial because it keeps you in a good frame of mind to continue to plan and teach at your best. An overwhelmed teacher is an unhappy teacher and an unhappy teacher has unhappy students. Clearly, this is best avoided.

Books

Only put work in the books when the marking will aid progress, otherwise use whiteboards or do it verbally. Marking takes up a lot of time; be wise about it. If the students can mark their own or each other's work, let them do so; just make sure it's done well.

Delegate

Where possible, delegate or share responsibility. All too often, we feel we have to do it or it won't be done right. Being a control freak is something that plagues many teachers, but so is fatigue. If you can share the load, do so. Maybe you can do some of the planning whilst a colleague organises the resources. Wherever you can, lighten the load.

Acceptance

Sometimes we just have to accept that it won't all get done. What's important is that the tasks that aren't done have the least impact on progress.

Relationships

Work on relationships with colleagues and students. If you get this right, everything else should follow.

Switching Off

Prioritise switching off. If you don't, you risk dealing with a complete lack of energy and enthusiasm which can result in resentment. It's too easy to work from eight o'clock in the morning until six o'clock in the evening at school and then continue marking and planning at home. Although this helps in the short term, it has many long term negative effects, especially with positivity.

Feeling Swamped

There are times when you have so much to do that you don't actually know where to start. My advice here is to take a deep breath, a step back and prioritise. Do whatever needs to be done first, even if you need to have a quick cup of tea in order to get your head around what that is.

Be Organised

Save yourself extra work in the long run by doing things properly in the first place. File paperwork properly, make sure your computer files are clear and easy to work out and keep your classroom organised. Remember, you are leading by example.

Be a Learner Again

Learn something new. Join a choir, learn a language, do a dance class

– anything to put you back in the place of the student and stimulate positive energy. You'll feel in a better place to deal with students if you've spent time doing things you enjoy rather than constantly working. You'll also remember what it feels like to be a learner again!

Be Effective

Spend your time effectively. Long hours do not always equal great teaching, in fact they can have exactly the opposite effect. Use the internet to help you with resources. Before creating anything new, always search for it online first – the chances are that someone has already done it and saved you the time. If a colleague can show you how to do something faster or has a particular strength that would help you become more effective, seek them out, ask for help and offer something in return. It's more than likely that there's something you can help them with too!

Remember:
Prioritise
Plan Accordingly
Books
Delegate
Acceptance
Relationships
Switching Off
Feeling Swamped

Be Organised

Be a Learner Again

Be Effective

Never re-invent the wheel, always save your work, share resources
with colleagues and do things properly in the first place.
Act purposefully. In everything.

Having a Bad Day

*"Success is going from failure to failure without losing your
enthusiasm."*

\- Winston Churchill

On a good day, teaching can be one of the best jobs in the world. On
a bad day, it can seem like one of the worst. And there will be bad
days. The key is realising that it is just that and dealing with it
accordingly.

Share Experiences

Regularly go into the staff room and share experiences with
colleagues; you'll discover that they have very similar experiences.
Organise a timetabled line management meeting where you can get
support and be honest with someone who can coach you properly. Let
the stress go; it does you no favours to hold onto it. As Bill Rogers

advises, think of any negative incidents as a small black dot on a large white page in order to put it into perspective. Tom Sherrington has a good blog entry about it here: http://headguruteacher.com/2013/01/06/behaviour-management-a-bill-rogers-top-10/)

Self-reflection

Although it is important to reflect, don't be too hard on yourself. Remember there's always something to work on, no matter who you are or what you do. None of us are perfect, even if, because you've stepped into a teaching role, people expect you to be. The main purpose of our lives is to be happy, that goes for our students too. It is important to remind ourselves of that sometimes.

Focus on the Positives

Focussing on the positives should be easy given that teaching can be one of the most rewarding jobs on the planet. Unfortunately, it's usually the negative that sticks with us. Train yourself from the start to think about the positives so that it becomes habit. Rather than focussing on one troublesome student, focus on the other twenty nine who respond well. Staying with that good energy, led by good intention, will bring you success.

Remember:

Share Experiences

Self-reflection

Focus on the Positives

If all else fails, drink tea and eat chocolate. Or do whatever you need to do to feel good again.

Intention

"Our intention creates our reality."

-Wayne Dyer

Intention is our driving force, our reason for doing, and in teaching (as well as in life) we need to be clear what our intention is. For a few years, my intention wasn't right. It was for me to do well, to please my superiors. I did okay; I had a mix of good and outstanding grades, but I also had no work-life balance and wanted to leave the profession. Now my intention is different. It is for my students to do well. As a consequence, I no longer do anything unless it adds significant value to the learning. I am now more effective. My students do well and, as a side effect, I'm respected for my work and receive consistent grade ones in observations. The students can tell when they are your main focus and respond well to it, the energy you give being the energy you receive. Try to enjoy and be positive about what you do because the enjoyment and positivity will spread.

Teaching is an intense profession because you are dealing with people. No matter how well planned you are, you can never be one hundred per cent sure that it will go as you believe it will. You never know for sure what mood the students are going to be in, what has happened to them the night before or whether they are looking forward to/are worrying about something that is going to happen the next day. All you can do is be consistent, a teacher whose high expectations are clear and a teacher who cares.

The one definite aim is for your students to make progress. Use this guide as and when you need it to provide you with tips and strategies to benefit your practice. If you would like more in-depth information, look for more titles that will be published in this series; each one will focus on one aspect of teaching so you can choose an area you would like to expand upon.

In this profession, we are always learning and adapting; it's what makes it such an interesting career. That and, of course, the students.

I wish you all the best.

Printed in Great Britain
by Amazon.co.uk, Ltd.,
Marston Gate.